Oration on the Unveiling of the Statue of Samuel Francis DuPont

Also from Westphalia Press
westphaliapress.org

Oration on the Unveiling of the Statue of Samuel Francis DuPont
Rear Admiral, U.S.N., at Washington, DC
on
December 20, 1884

by Hon. Thomas F. Bayard

WESTPHALIA PRESS
An imprint of Policy Studies Organization

An imprint of Policy Studies Organization
1527 New Hampshire Ave., NW
Washington, D.C. 20036
info@ipsonet.org

ISBN-13: 978-1-63391-186-4
ISBN-10: 1633911861

Cover design by Taillefer Long at Illuminated Stories:
www.illuminatedstories.com

Daniel Gutierrez-Sandoval, Executive Director
PSO and Westphalia Press

Updated material and comments on this edition
can be found at the Westphalia Press website:
www.westphaliapress.org

ORATION

ON THE

UNVEILING OF THE STATUE

OF

SAMUEL FRANCIS DuPONT,

REAR ADMIRAL, U. S. N.,

AT WASHINGTON, D. C., DEC. 20TH, 1884,

BY

HON. THOMAS F. BAYARD,

UNITED STATES SENATOR FROM DELAWARE.

ORATION

UNVEILING OF THE STATUE

OF

SAMUEL FRANCIS DuPONT,

REAR ADMIRAL, U. S. N.,

AT WASHINGTON, D. C., DEC. 20TH, 1884,

BY

HON. THOMAS F. BAYARD,

UNITED STATES SENATOR FROM DELAWARE.

WILMINGTON, DEL.
PRESS OF FERRIS BROS., PRINTERS.
1885.

PREFATORY NOTE.

By an act approved February 25th, 1882, Congress provided that "the circle at the intersection of Massachusetts and Connecticut avenues," in this city, should be called "DuPont Circle," and ten thousand dollars were appropriated for the "preparation of the circle and of the base for a proposed statue of Rear-Admiral Samuel Francis DuPont, to be erected thereon." The act of Congress approved March 3, 1884, provided that the "unexpended balance ($3,200) of the sum appropriated under" the first-mentioned act, "together with the further sum of ten thousand five hundred dollars," should be expended for the "erection and completion of a statue" of Rear-Admiral DuPont, "to be placed in DuPont Circle, in the city of Washington. The sundry civil appropriation act, approved July 7th, 1884, contained a provision by which the sum of five hundred dollars was appropriated to "defray the expenses attending the unveiling of the statue." This amount, together with the sums previously mentioned, was to be expended under the direction of the Secretary of War.

The statue, modeled by Mr. Launt Thompson, of New York, was erected early in December, 1884, and accepted by the Hon. Robert T. Lincoln, Secretary of War. The arrangements for the ceremony of unveiling the statue were made, under the direction of the Hon. William E. Chandler, Secretary of the Navy, by a committee composed of Vice-Admiral Stephen C. Rowan, Rear-Admirals John L. Worden, C. R. P. Rodgers, and Clark H. Wells, and Surgeon-General

Francis M. Gunnell. Commander Bowman H. McCalla was charged with the immediate supervision of the ceremony.

The statue was unveiled on the 20th of December, 1884, in the presence of the President of the United States and the members of the Cabinet, members of both houses of Congress, and officers of the Army and Navy. All officers of the regular and volunteer services who had served under Admiral DuPont, either in the Mexican war or in the war of the Union, were specially invited to witness the ceremony. A special invitation was also sent to Mrs. DuPont, the widow of the late admiral, who was, however, unable to come to Washington. Among the other invited guests, there were present twenty members of the DuPont family, and sixty members of "Admiral S. F. DuPont Post, No. 2," Grand Army of the Republic, of Wilmington, Delaware.

A detachment, composed of seamen from the U. S. S. Despatch, and of marines from the navy-yard, was drawn up to the right and left of the statue.

The ceremony began at 2.15 p. m. with the opening address of the Secretary of the Navy.

Prayer was offered by the Rev. W. A. Leonard, of Washington.

At a signal from the Secretary of the Navy, the statue was unveiled by two petty officers of the Despatch, the seamen and marines presenting arms, and the drums rolling twice.

The oration was delivered by the Hon. Thos. F. Bayard, United States Senator from Delaware.

At the conclusion of the oration a rear-admiral's salute of thirteen guns was fired by the light battery of the Second Regiment, United States Artillery.

OPENING ADDRESS

HON. WILLIAM E. CHANDLER,

SECRETARY OF THE NAVY.

———

We have assembled to honor the memory of one of the naval heroes of the war of the Union—Samuel Francis Du-Pont—who entered the Navy in 1815, a boy of twelve, and died in the service in 1865, a rear-admiral. His faithful labors for his country, his patience, dignity, and loyalty under trying circumstances, and his important achievements in battle against the enemy, have made his name illustrious.

The Congress has ordered that his statue shall be here erected, an enduring memorial of his virtues, his valor, and his patriotism.

PRAYER

REV. WILLIAM A. LEONARD.

O Lord, our Heavenly Father, the high and mighty ruler of the universe, who dost from Thy throne behold all the dwellers upon earth, we humbly beseech Thee to send down upon this special service of earthly reward and commemoration Thy heavenly benediction.

Accept our hearty thanks for the good life and good example of Thy servant, whom to-day we honor; whose course of faith and duty here being finished, now rests from his labors. Raise up and indue with power and virtue, integrity and Christian heroism, such as shall serve their country and Thee in all holiness and courage. Grant peace in our time, O Lord, and victory always to the hosts that fight against ignorance and sin, and in the cause of right and truth. Bless and protect from all dangers those who go down to the sea in ships, and teach them their dependence on Thy almighty arm, and build us up as Thy people, Thy loyal, faithful helpers, so that we may receive Thy blessing here, and Thy peace hereafter, through Jesus Christ, our Savior, who hath taught us say: Our Father which art in Heaven, hallowed be Thy name. Thy kingdom come. Thy will be done on earth, as it is in heaven. Give us this day our daily bread, and forgive us our trespasses as we forgive those who trespass against us. And lead us not into temptation, but deliver us from evil; for Thine is the kingdom, and the power, and the glory, for ever and ever. Amen.

ORATION.

THE statue just unveiled to our view attests the gratitude of a republic — of a great family of republics acting in a national union. It has been erected under the authority of the Congress of the United States, and to-day, in our presence, has been consecrated by prayer to the Almighty Ruler of the Universe, and is now dedicated in perpetuation of the name, fame, and memory of Samuel Francis DuPont, a rear admiral in the navy of the United States, who, from the date of his appointment as a midshipman, on December 19, 1815, until his death, on June 23, 1865, rendered devoted and faithful service to the people of the United States and their government.

Early in the present year, in conformity with the law, the execution of the work was placed under the direction of the Honorable Secretary of War, and with his approval confided to Mr. Launt Thompson, of New York city.

The result of his skill and labor now stands before us in a figure of bronze, of heroic proportions, moulded in an attitude natural to the man whom it admirably represents.

The pedestal of grey granite, designed also by Mr. Thompson, rests upon a base of blue rock from the hills of the Brandywine, in the State of Delaware, the scene of the the early youth and all of the home life of Admiral DuPont. The artist has not only been fortunate in producing a likeness declared excellent by the family and friends of his subject, but in his representation of characteristic attitude and expression has admirably combined truth to nature with fidelity to art.

The admiral is here represented as standing on the quarter deck, marine glass in hand, which he has just lowered after an inspection of a distant object, leaving his countenance lit with an expression of alert interest. It may be accepted as a vivid and realistic reproduction and portrayal of a frequent incident in his daily life, when in command of the blockading squadron off the south Atlantic coast, in which duty unrelaxed vigilance was required. He is represented in the uniform of the period, and of his rank in the naval service. The artist has indeed been fortunate in his subject, and is entitled to congratulation for the ability with which he has availed himself of his great opportunity.

A description of the personal appearance of Admiral DuPont, drawn near the close of his latest active service by the pen of one who knew him long and intimately, and was one of his most distinguished companions-in-arms, Rear Admiral Daniel Ammen, may be here appropriately given: " In appearance he was distinguished, over six feet in height, admirably proportioned, graceful and urbane, with an intelligent expression and action. It will not be considered adulatory by those who knew him to say that no officer in our navy within the past half century was gifted with a more distinguished appearance or exalted character." Long and illustrious as is the roll of honor of the American navy, it is unjust to no name that adorns it to say that none has ever exhibited a more ingrained devotion, a more zealous and solicitous guardianship of its honor, interests, and efficiency than Samuel Francis DuPont, and the rapid summary of his life and services which I shall now essay will amply justify the testimonial of posthumous honor by his government which has caused us to assemble here.

He was the youngest son of Victor Marie DuPont and Gabrielle Josephine de la Fite de Pelleport, daughter of René, Marquis de Pelleport, and was born at Bergen Point, N. J., September 27, 1803. His father was born in Paris in 1767, entered upon a diplomatic career, had been attached to the French legation in the United States in 1787, and in 1795 became first secretary of that legation, and in the same year was appointed French consul at Charleston, S. C.,—a point long after made interesting in the history of his son. After two years service at Charleston he was appointed consul-general of France in the United States, but left the service and returned to France, whence he emigrated to the United States with his father, and finally settled permanently at Louviers, on the Brandywine, near Wilmington, Del., where he died in 1824.

Pierre Samuel DuPont de Nemours, the grandfather of the rear admiral, was a distinguished French economist, statesman, and writer, whose interest in the united American colonies was importantly manifested, and who finally became a citizen of the United States, and died in Delaware in 1817. He had rendered active service in the negotiation of the treaty between Great Britain and France in 1782, in which the independence of the United States was recognized, and in 1803 had been instrumental in the negotiation of a treaty with France under the administration of Mr. Jefferson, by which Louisiana was acquired by the United States. On both sides of his house Admiral DuPont was descended from an honorable and distinguished ancestry in France, whose descendants as citizens of the United States have maintained without blemish the high character of the race from which they sprung.

Shortly after his birth his parents removed to Louviers, a country seat in the vicinity of Wilmington, Del., and there, on the picturesque and healthful banks of the Brandywine, near the memorable field of battle of that name, in which the Marquis de la Fayette was seriously wounded, the early youth of the admiral was passed.   There was the home of his childhood and his affections, the scene of his manhood and married happiness, and there, in the maturity of his years and fame, his mortal frame was laid to rest.   He was married in 1833 to Miss Sophie M. DuPont, who still survives him, and has no children.   When but a mere child, little more than twelve years of age, on December 19, 1815, he received from President Madison his appointment as midshipman in the navy.   Almost simultaneously he was tendered a cadetship at West Point, but his preference was strongly for the navy, and, impressed with the traditions of his maternal ancestry, he entered at once upon a career of arms.

The interest of Thomas Jefferson in the family of his friend DuPont de Nemours, drew from him a letter upon this occasion, of which an extract at this date may be interesting:

"For twenty years to come we should consider peace as the *summum bonum* of our country.   By that time your grandson will have become one of our high admirals, and bear distinguished part in retorting the wrongs of both of his countries on the most implacable and cruel of their enemies.   In this hope, and because I love you and all who are dear to you, I wrote the President on the instant of reading your letter of the 7th on the subject of his adoption into our Navy.   I did it because I was gratified in doing it, while I knew it was unnecessary.   The sincere respect and high estimation in which the President holds you is such that there is no gratification within the regular exercise of his functions which he would withhold from you.   Be assured that if within that compass, the business is safe."

His sea service commenced forthwith, and he made his first voyage to the Mediterranean in the Franklin, seventy-four, under the command of the illustrious Commodore Charles Stewart.

By the courtesy of the Honorable Secretary of the Navy,

I have been supplied with an abstract of his official record in that Department, from the date of his entrance into the service as a midshipman, until his death, a rear admiral; and, interesting and valuable though it is, it is yet too long for insertion in these remarks. As a summary of this record I may state that from December, 1815, onward, in war and peace, afloat or ashore, he diligently, and with intervals of leisure few and of short duration, served his country until his death in June, 1865; for eleven years as a midshipman; for sixteen years as a lieutenant; for thirteen years as a commander; for seven years as a captain; and for three years as a rear-admiral; giving part even of his childhood, his entire youth, and the whole of his mature manhood, to faithful public service. A half century of human life dedicated to honor and usefulness, and illuminated by the practice and exhibition of the highest human qualities. Those who knew him longest and best will attest that he was ever self-subordinating, self-respecting, prompt, and cheerful in the performance of duty and the execution of the commands of his official superiors; diligent in self-cultivation and study, ardent in the acquirement of professional knowledge in every branch, rigid in the enforcement of discipline, but merciful and just in the exercise of authority; gentle, generous, courteous, and considerate of his associates and official inferiors; courageous in the face of danger; sensitive alike of his personal honor, and the honor of his flag; spirited in resenting indignity or disrespect; conscientious, self-reliant, and responsible in council and decision. I have read a letter written near the close of his career to the Secretary of the Navy, which so well illustrates these latter qualities that I have transcribed it:

"I did not hold a council of war, either before or after the attack, nor have I ever held a council of war in my life. I did not desire to throw upon the gallant officers who commanded the iron-clads, and who had so nobly borne themselves in this novel mode of warfare, any of the responsibilities which pertained to my own station, and I did not hear their opinions as to the withdrawal of the fleet until I had announced my own determination in the matter."

These were the living principles of his action, and they were accompanied and strengthened by his devout and humble profession and practice as a Christian, which led him into an active and consistent membership of the Protestant Episcopal church.

The range and varied nature of his service seem unbounded. He carried the flag of his country on the high seas into the four quarters of the globe, everywhere and at all times maintaining with dignity and punctilious care the national honor and the reputation of the service. A love of the Navy and a thorough knowledge of its needs grew into his life and became part of his very being. The tender and impressible age at which he entered the Navy had much to do with this, and the great law of gradual growth was well expressed in him, as he rose from rank to rank, unfolding higher capacities at each step, until he became, in the judgment of those most competent to speak, a thorough sailor, skilled in every branch of his profession. A noble emulation filled him, and by study and careful self-cultivation he attained that proficiency in languages and polite literature which marked his public reports and correspondence, and distinguished him in official and social intercourse. His fine presence, voice, and manners proclaimed that he possessed

> All, that when language slow the thought imparts,
> Comes in that one word "sailor" to our hearts.

In every field of duty, on sea or land, he was found ever energetic, courageous, conscientious in the performance of duty; from 1815 to 1845, in active sea service in all quarters, in men-of-war of well-known repute, the companion and cherished friend of officers whose names are historic and honored.

Upon the founding of the Naval School at Annapolis, under the administration of the Navy Department, by the Hon. George Bancroft, he assisted Commodore Franklin Buchanan in organizing the school, and very shortly was transferred to the Congress of the Pacific squadron, Commodore Stockton commanding, and was again transferred to the command of the Cyane in July, 1846.

The conquest of California having been effected by the squadron under Commodore Stockton, the Cyane was employed in blockade duty on the west coast of Mexico, and in cruising in the Gulf of California.

The exploits of the Cyane under DuPont's command on the Mexican coast form a brilliant chapter in the history of that war. In fact, the conduct of the entire naval force on that station was worthy of the best traditions of American seamanship, enterprise, and courage. Its influence upon the campaign has scarcely received its due appreciation, and its effect upon the prestige and reputation of the Navy was great and permanent.

Commander DuPont returned in the Cyane to Norfolk in October, 1848, after three years of constant and efficient service, having, notwithstanding long blockades at anchor and defence of harbors, sailed sixty-five thousand miles. The long list of prizes captured, of vessels of the enemy and property destroyed by them to avoid capture, of cities subdued and ports blockaded by his energy and enterprise, has found honorable record in the files of the Navy Department. His personal gallantry flashed out on many occasions during this campaign, as when he landed one hundred of his officers and crew in the face of a military force of all arms immensely superior, and at the head of his little band fought his way through many times their number and relieved the brave Lieutenant Heywood and his heroic garrison in the mission-house of San José, where he had been beleaguered and brought to great distress. The dispatches of Lieutenant Heywood and Commodore Shubrick contain vivid descriptions of the fiery courage of DuPont in this affair. Equally discreet and prudent as courageous, we find no disaster to the public property, nor want of care of the health or the lives of the officers or the men intrusted to his command. In the various affairs in which the Cyane was engaged in the cruise off Mexico, she lost seventeen killed and wounded, and out of a crew of two hundred and ten men but a single death from sickness occurred. After his return in the Cyane, Captain DuPont was employed as examiner of midshipmen and reviser of the rules of the Naval School. He became a member of the Light-House Board, and combined with this important service the command of the receiving ship at Philadelphia. In 1855 he became a member of the board to promote the efficiency of the Navy, and upon him as an ardent friend to the reform fell the main weight of painful responsibilities in the execution of this expurgating law. " The cankers of a calm world and a long peace" needed excision, and the surgery was necessarily sharp and painful. It drew upon Captain DuPont a great amount of personal and bitter hostility from the officers unfavorably affected by the law, when the names of the individuals selected for retirement, by reason of supposed disability and unfitness, were made known. His popularity in the Navy, which up to that time had been well nigh universal, at once lessened, and he was compelled to face a whirlwind of disappointed ambition, denunciation, and even personal slander and vilification. But he was in the path of duty, and he stood fast until the storm spent its force, leaving him shocked and saddened by its violence, but erect, and true to his convictions, with not a stain upon his reputation, and the arrows of defamation lying shattered at his feet. But this was a painful and deeply trying episode in his career, and it left some wounds which were slow in healing. He was two years in command of the Minnesota in the East India squadron, and returned home to serve upon boards of examination and in command of the Philadelphia navy-yard.

In September, 1861, he was ordered to the command of the South Atlantic blockading squadron, and in the following month of June, was promoted to the rank of rear-admiral, and continued in the same command.

The war to prevent the secession of the Southern States closed, so far as armed hostilities were concerned, in the spring of 1865, a few months before the death of Admiral DuPont. It embraced in the period of its continuance a memorable era in the history of maritime warfare, and developed new theories and practice in naval architecture and armament, which to-day, while abolishing as with a wave of the hand of inexorable fate the wooden-built navies of the world, leaves uncertain and unsettled what shall permanently succeed them.

As touching the career and character of the naval officer we are now considering, this wonderful and deeply interesting fact may be considered pertinent.

Up to Saturday, the 8th day of March, 1862, when the Merrimac, the first iron-clad of any type, came out of Norfolk harbor, and under the guns of Fortress Monroe ravaged with impunity the shipping, armed and unarmed, in Hampton Roads, the Navy of the United States had been believed to contain vessels of war of the highest type, and the equals in their respective classes of any other navy. On the evening of the same day the Monitor, the first iron-clad of her own type, the offspring of the genius of Ericsson, arrived in Hampton Roads, and the next day presented herself to the Merrimac in defense of the wooden frigate Minnesota, up to that time considered a formidable man-of-war, but in the presence of the Merrimac proved to be a defenceless victim.

In the desperate and critical battle that then took place in Hampton Roads the end of wooden navies was decreed, but what was to take their place was and still remains undecided. This remarkable sea fight was no mere test of manœuvres of navigation and scientific target practice; it was the *experimentum crucis* of veritable war, waged under conditions and with instruments and methods theretofore almost unknown, and wholly untested,—a death-grapple of skill, backed by courage unsurpassed, and sealing its convictions in wounds and death. The terrible earnestness of this encounter disclosed the true features of the new departure in maritime warfare, and so sudden and sweeping a revolution had never before been wrought in history. It proved much, but not all, and in the sequel much that is tragical has occurred. The pathway to complete success is often paved with failure and suffering. The Monitor—whose name is inseparable from that of Ericsson, whose genius devised her; of Worden, whose heroism tested her; and of Green, who caught up the torch of glory as it dropped from the hand of Worden, when he fell blinded and bleeding in the combat—came in a few months to a pitiable end.

In December following, the Monitor, having been thoroughly repaired, endeavored to find her way, under tow, from the capes of the Chesapeake to Charleston, to participate in the contemplated attack on that city, and in a mere capful of wind went helplessly to the bottom of the sea off Cape Hatteras. The Weehawken, at her moorings in Charleston harbor, in fair weather, went down in five minutes after her first signal for assistance was given.

Contributions of disaster to heavily-armored war-ships come from the English navy: the Captain, a marvel of impregnability, sunk in the Bay of Biscay, with her freight of five hundred officers and men, and the handful of half-drowned survivors were never able satisfactorily to account for what had happened; the Vanguard, armor-plated, collided with no especial violence with her consort, and sank instantly in the Irish Sea. And the problem of weight and strength *versus* security and efficiency remains unsolved.

In the winter of 1861, in attempted secrecy, but with anxious haste, the skill and ingenuity of Americans on either side, in the ship-yards at Brooklyn and Norfolk, were quietly maturing inventions which were to be the main factors in deciding the great contest.

The Merrimac and the Monitor were the pioneers in the new system of naval warfare, the offspring on either side of American skill, and tested equally by the courage of American seamen. The combat between these two vessels ended wooden fleets, although as yet wooden cruisers may be temporarily in use, for this has now become the "age of steel."

In November, 1861, Commodore DuPont had safely and skillfully carried his fleet of wooden ships, led by his flag-ship, the Wabash, into the waters of Port Royal Harbor; and with masterly skill, handling his fleet with perfect regularity, and his guns with a fatal precision never surpassed in naval operations, had reduced earthworks of great strength, defended by guns of superior calibre, manned with skill and courage. With celerity and unchecked success he had accomplished all and more than the task allotted to him, and had conquered and secured an admirable base of supplies, and of naval and military operations, most advantageous to the Government and dangerous to the enemy.

Seamanship, comprehensive military judgment, intelligent and aggressive warfare, were never better illustrated than by him in this expedition. A paper blockade was succeeded by a rigorous blockade *de facto*, and a long line of coast, with its adjacent rivers and harbors, fell under the control of the United States, and so continued.

All this had been accomplished with the instrumentalities known to naval warfare up to the spring of 1862. But the methods and instruments of maritime war were now to give way to the novel inventions, and the latter were pressed forward in the midst of delighted surprise and excitement, without a careful estimate of their real capacities or of their serious defects. Yet in this juncture the ability and ready, well-disciplined intelligence of the officers of the American Navy were admirably displayed, and they quickly recognized all that had taken place, and addressed all their faculties to the new work before them. It is not to be wondered at, that, reacting from the almost hopeless horror which the appearance of the Merrimac and her resistless power caused in the minds and hearts of those who witnessed them, and all to whom such tidings came north of the scene of action, the unexpected arrival, as in special benediction, of the Monitor, and the unhesitating courage with which her commander, the gallant Worden, interposed his untried and experimental craft to meet the onslaught of her terrible and mysterious antagonist, won for vessel and commander a gratitude, applause, and admiration well deserved, but which led to a hasty over-valuation of the type of such vessels, which has had many unhappy results. There was much excitement and a popular demand for success; and for a time reason seemed to have been swept away from the people, and cool judgment from the administration, and employment was demanded for which such vessels had no adaptation, and results confidently expected which could never be realized. The clamor for an iron-clad fleet of the Monitor type became at once loud and widespread, and was yielded to by the Navy Department in such a degree that Mr. Fox, the Assistant Secretary, told Admiral DuPont that "one monitor alone would cause the immediate evacuation of Charleston."

The construction of such vessels was at once vigorously begun; and although many improvements were made, and obvious defects in the original model avoided, yet the inherent unfitness of such vessels for cruising at sea, or to be handled readily in narrow channels, or even for living with safety in rough water, could not be and never has been remedied. The careful judgments of the most able and experienced officers in the Navy, and their representations of the imperfections of these vessels, the dangers attending their employment, and their unfitness for the serious task proposed for them, were all overborne by the volubility of interested contractors, with their usual vociferous escort of political " pot-hunters." The elements of resistance in the Navy Department were not then sufficiently strong, so that seven iron vessels of the Monitor type, and another, the New Ironsides, better planned and more seaworthy, were rapidly finished and sent down to the South Atlantic squadron to execute the Department decree, that Charleston must be attacked by them, and that the attack must be successful. Against these plans Admiral DuPont's judgment was opposed; but other influences proved too strong for the acceptance of his counsel. He wrote to the Department:

" The powers and adaptability of these vessels were as much a sealed book to me as the defences of Charleston to the Department; but under all circumstances, to wit, the imperfect knowledge of those defences and of the powers of iron-clads, in which the Department had expressed unbounded confidence, no officer could hesitate to make the experiment, and I gave to it my whole heart and energy, not hesitating to ask the Department for all the iron-clads that could be spared, and I am happy to say that the Department spared no pains to increase the force of those vessels. * * * and in my dispatch No. 41, written as early as January 28, 1863, I expressed myself as follows:

" ' My own previous impressions of these vessels, frequently expressed to Assistant Secretary Fox, have been confirmed, viz., that whatever degree of impenetrability they might have, there was no corresponding quality of aggression or destructiveness as against forts.   * * * *

" ' This experiment also convinced me of another impression, firmly held and often expressed, that in all such operations, to secure success, troops are necessary.'

"These facts, however, seemed not to have changed the views of the Department, and in accordance with its previous orders and its well-known determination to effect the capture of Charleston, I determined to make the experiment, and to risk and probably lose whatever of prestige pertained to a long and successful professional career, in order to meet the necessities of war and the wishes of the Government."

There is no time now and here for a description of the attack of the fleet of iron-clads on Charleston. It proved to be a failure, but his self-reliant and courageous judgment ordered the withdrawal of the fleet when the proper moment arrived, in order, as he wrote, to "prevent a failure from being converted into a disaster," and with the intention to renew the attack the next day; but so furious had been the contest, so vigorous and stubborn the resistance, as well as the persistent intrepidity of the attack, that upon calling his commanders to report on the evening after the battle, it was discovered that five out of the eight vessels were disabled, and that "half an hour more fighting would have placed them all *hors de combat.*" The Keokuk, an iron-plated vessel, sank the next morning at daybreak from the injuries received.

Read by the light of the facts as we now know them, it becomes difficult to measure the value to the cause in which he was engaged of the judgment and decision of Admiral DuPont at this juncture. The scope of the "disaster" so alluded to, consequent upon the eight ironclads falling into the hands of the enemy whilst in a disabled condition, it may be well to consider. The possession of such vessels at that time by the enemy would have put an end to the entire blockade by wooden vessels, and the unprotected condition of the seaboard of the Northern States (which unhappily is suffered to continue) would have made a widespread devastation in that quarter speedily possible. With the blockade so broken, the action of foreign governments in respect to the recognition of the new confederacy might have given a turn to events not pleasant for contemplation even at this remote date. Yet these suggestions may assist in measuring the responsibility of the commanding officer, the soundness of his opinions given to the Navy Department, and the value of his judicious conduct in ordering the attack to come to an end just when he did, thereby preventing a " disaster" grave indeed, and whose far-reaching consequences it is difficult for the imagination to limit.

There is not, in my opinion, a public virtue more valuable, and unfortunately more rare, than the deliverance of judgments in a period of adverse popular excitement. And yet just then fidelity is most needed, and the expression of real convictions.

When Admiral DuPont's duty required the delivery of his judgment as to the practicability of capturing Charleston with the new fleet of iron-clads, and without the co-operative movement of a strong land force, he gave it sincerely, and preferred to displease rather than mislead the public and those who had intrusted him with the command. As I read his dispatches, the more I feel his fame and memory deserve this public recognition, for he possessed the qualities that save nations—those personal qualities that are indeed the pivots upon which the great wheels of human society securely and smoothly revolve, and which all political societies need for their safety in the high places of public trust. Wordsworth expresses well the thought.

> Say, what is honor ? 'Tis the finest sense
> Of justice which the human mind can frame.

And this man had honor—sneered at by the base and shallow as a mere abstraction, but which will prove in the great stress and strain of events the most absolute and important reality. It was this that impelled Admiral DuPont to tell unpalatable truths in an hour of excitement, when great results were pending. He was overborne, and his great heart was pained, and his high and delicate pride wounded by injustice, ignorance, aspersion, and the other countless shafts against which no coat of mail can protect. But time was his vindicator, and the correctness of his judgment was soon established. His successor in command, Rear-Admiral Dahlgren, an officer of high attainments and courage, never attempted a course of action different from his predecessor, and in his published memoir ample material will be found—if it were needed—wholly to exonerate Admiral DuPont and to justify the counsel he gave and the action he pursued. The history of the Navy from that day to this attests the truth of all he reported, and since he led the fleet of iron-clad monitors to the assault upon the defences of Charleston, no renewal of the attack was ever ordered or made, and no other vessel of the type has been put in service.

Thus it became the conspicuous and historical duty of this distinguished officer, near the close of his career, to give brilliant and instructive illustration of professional ability alike in the old and in the new methods of naval warfare; to lead into action the last fleet of wooden vessels and the first fleet of iron-clads.

In both enterprises his conduct was eminently skillful and courageous, and in both he had the able co-operation of commanding officers, of whom he wrote to the Department:

"They have been long known to me; many of them served in the squadron before, and were present at the capture of the Port Royal forts. They are men of the highest professional capacity and courage, and fully sustained their reputation."

And he goes on to name them; and when and where can those names ever be better repeated than now, in association with his own?

Commodore Thomas Turner, of the New Ironsides; Captain Percival Drayton, of the Passaic; Captain John Rodgers, of the Weehawken; Captain John L. Worden, of the Montauk; Commander Daniel Ammen, of the Patapsco; Commander George W. Rodgers, of the Catskill; Commander D. M'N. Fairfax, of the Nantucket; Commander John Downes, of the Nahant; and Commander A. C. Rhind, of the Keokuk.

And describing the "invaluable assistance" of his Fleet Captain, Commander C. R. P. Rodgers, he says, "For now over eighteen months this officer has been afloat with me, and in my opinion no language could overstate his services to his country, to his fleet, and to myself as his commander-in-chief."

With such companions-in-arms well might he express gratification in receiving their "unanimous and cordial" support, and confirmation in the responsible judgments he delivered in a season of grave peril to the cause in which he and they were engaged.

The proper scope of this address does not admit a more detailed biography of the officer in whose honor this statue is erected. In saying what I have, it has been my intention only to describe the man as he lived, and the circumstances which surrounded him, which tested and proved the qualities he possessed, and entitle him to be perpetuated in the respectful and affectionate remembrance of his countrymen; that the generation who knew him may feel gratified by the just reward his name receives; that the youth who are now upon the threshold of life may find in his character and career an example and incentive to pursue with earnest devotion the path of rugged duty, until they gather on the table-lands of truth the sweet flower of honor and the loftier crown of Divine approval.

Our age is one of utility, and our lives in this new and vast country are filled with ceaseless activity in the creation and acquisition of material wealth, so that society needs

other and counteracting forces to free us from sordid influences and lead us to higher and better lives. Encourage-
ment must be given to pursuits that have not wealth as their
aim or reward. There must be an incentive to our youth

To scorn delights and live laborious days,

and this it is a public duty to supply. Education will ex-
pand the horizon of knowledge, and learning will increase
the intellectual demands ; and knowledge will supply means
for their gratification; and the mind and soul will thus
rise above the grossness of material life, and a progress
upward as well as onward will mark American civilization.
Public respect and recognition of virtue exhibited for the
public welfare should be generously and gratefully bestowed.
Nothing should be omitted that can mould public opinion to
award honor and praise to those who have served worthily
and are entitled to the palm of public favor.

The night before the battle of Aboukir Bay, Nelson
said to his officers, " Before this time to-morrow I shall have
gained a peerage or Westminster Abbey." Such were the
rewards which his heroic spirit sought. A peerage officers
of the United States are forbidden to receive, nor have we
as yet in our new land a venerable repository for the ashes
and memories of our distinguished dead; but there are public
buildings fit to receive the statues of those who have well
served the Republic in any calling, and no place so proper
as this city, the seat and centre of the Government of the
United States. The erection of this statue is in the line
of public justice and proper recognition of the unselfish devotion of the individual to the welfare of the community.
Approval of this public act of justice will be widespread
in this broad land, but nowhere so strong as in the State
in which the ashes of her heroic son are deposited.

The State of Delaware has given to the United States
Navy men on whose brows the laurels of victory have justly

rested. The victory on Lake Champlain was gained by one of her sons, Commodore McDonough, and in the severest battles of the same same war with Great Britain, another, Commodore Jacob Jones, stood in the front rank of honor. From the earliest confederation of the American colonies Delaware has borne an honorable and faithful part in the " common defence and general welfare," and to-day the hearts of her people are filled with gratitude in this recognition by the General Government of one of her citizens, so proudly cherished and beloved in life and mourned in death as Rear Admiral Samuel Francis DuPont.